PAINT
FINISHES

PAINT
FINISHES

Sacha Cohen

LORENZ BOOKS

This edition is published by Lorenz Books,
an imprint of Anness Publishing Ltd,
Blaby Road, Wigston,
Leicestershire LE18 4SE;

info@anness.com

www.lorenzbooks.com;
www.annesspublishing.com

If you like the images in this book
and would like to investigate using
them for publishing, promotions or
advertising, please visit our website
www.practicalpictures.com
for more information.

A CIP catalogue record for this book is
available from the British Library.

Publisher: Joanna Lorenz
Art Manager: Clare Reynolds
Editors: Felicity Forster, Anne Hildyard
Photographers: Lucinda Symons,
    Rodney Forte & John Freeman
Designer: Bill Mason
Production Controller: Pirong Wang
Additional text: Mike Lawrence

PUBLISHER'S NOTE
The author and publishers have made
every effort to ensure that all instructions
contained within this book are accurate and
safe, and cannot accept liability for any
resulting injury, damage or loss to persons
or property, however it may arise. If in any
doubt as to the correct procedure to follow
for any home improvements task, seek
professional advice.

CONTENTS

INTRODUCTION

For many people, decorating with paint means nothing more than applying solid colours to their walls, ceilings and woodwork, but there is so much more to be achieved with paint if a few techniques are learned and a little imagination applied. There are many types of paint to choose from, never mind the vast kaleidoscope of colours, and you may be surprised at the variety of effects that are possible. What's more, decorating with paint allows you to create unique, one-off decorative effects that you could never achieve with other materials, such as wallpaper. And, when the time comes for a new look, paint is the quickest to prepare and the easiest of materials to cover with something fresh.

There are many types of decorative

paint effect to choose from, some being more difficult to create than others, but all are well within the scope of the determined and competent do-it-yourselfer. They can be applied to a variety of surfaces, but some lend themselves particularly to large areas, such as walls, while others are more

ABOVE: Colourwashing is a simple technique for applying an overall pattern to a large surface area; it can be done with a brush or sponge.

LEFT: In roller fidgeting, two different colours are applied by the same roller in one operation to give an interesting two-tone effect.

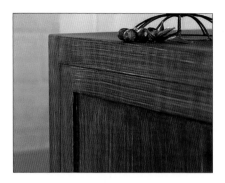

effective on smaller items, such as pieces of furniture.

Among the simplest of paint effects is the application of one colour over another in such a manner that the first can show through in some areas, usually in a random pattern. That pattern is created by using a variety of applicators – thick-bristled brushes, sponges or balls of cloth – and mixing additives into the paint that make it hold the marks that these leave.

More uniform patterns can be produced by using stencils or stamps to print motifs on the wall, or by masking certain areas before painting them. There are techniques, too, for painting surfaces to look like natural materials, such as wood or marble. These require a degree of skill, but can be achieved with practice and confidence.

Naturally, as with any painted finish, thorough preparation is crucial for any decorative paint effect; surfaces must always be sound and clean, while choosing the right tools is a must (some effects require special tools).

RIGHT: Trompe l'oeil effects are intended to deceive the eye into thinking that a flat surface has depth. Clouds provide a tranquil backdrop.

The type of paint you use is important too, since all have specific properties that make them suitable for particular situations. Knowing what you can and cannot do with a paint is vital.

In this book, not only will you learn about the tools and materials you need, but also a variety of decorative paint techniques, ranging from simple sponging to complex woodgraining and marbling. Study them carefully and use your imagination to choose the right ones for your situation. If you follow the step-by-step techniques, you will be able to give your home a new look that reflects your personality in a unique manner.

MATERIALS & PREPARATION

The most important requirement for successful results in paint effects is the proper use of the correct materials and tools. With many of the techniques you can achieve stunning decoration with ordinary household paintbrushes, rollers, sponges and artists' brushes, but special equipment is needed for some effects. These items are available in decorators' suppliers and craft shops, where you can also ask for advice on their use. Choose good-quality materials. Make sure that you have the right type of paint for the specific technique you are planning. Read carefully through the steps to check that you have everything you need before you start.

BASIC KIT

There are some basic essentials that you will need for decorating. You can add to this equipment gradually as you work on different effects.

Use a sturdy set of steps to reach the tops of walls and ceilings easily.

Buy dust sheets (drop cloths) to protect the floor, furniture and anything precious. Cotton twill dust sheets are reusable and preferable to the plastic-sheet disposable kind.

You may sometimes have to remove door furniture or wall fixings, so both Phillips and flat-blade screwdrivers are useful. They are also handy for removing paint can lids.

For general painting, edging and painting woodwork, use household paintbrushes. The most useful sizes are 5cm (2in) and 2.5cm (1in). Finer artists' brushes are invaluable for difficult small spaces and touching up odd areas. Soft

sable-haired artists' brushes with rounded edges are best for this use.

Fill any chipped areas with interior-grade filler (spackle or wood filler), applied with a filling knife. When dry, sand to a smooth finish.

It is sensible to use a paint kettle. Pour the paint into the kettle a little at a time so that it is not too heavy. Also, in case of accident the spillage will not be so great.

Use abrasive paper to key and prepare previously painted woodwork. It is generally best used with a sanding block for a flatter finish.

After sanding and prior to painting or staining, use a brush or cloth to dust away the sanded particles.

BELOW: When painting walls and ceilings, lay down a dust sheet (drop cloth) to protect the floor from accidental paint splashes.

BRUSHES

Numerous types, sizes and qualities of brush are available for different techniques. The brush must hold the required quantity of paint, be the correct size for the surface area and be made from the right type of hair. Natural hair and bristle brushes are best, but synthetic alternatives are less expensive and can give good results.

Use a graining brush for certain woodgrain effects. These are available in different sizes and with varying "pencils" or clumps of bristles.

Softener (blending) brushes have soft bristles with rounded ends. Large ones are used for softening basic finishes and the first layers of faux effects. Smaller ones are used for fine softening. The best ones are made from badger hair. Use a large soft blusher brush as a cheap alternative.

Dragging brushes are used for woodgraining and dragged effects. They are usually about 5cm (2in) or 7.5cm (3in) wide.

CLEANING BRUSHES

Wash brushes in soapy water if using a water-based (latex) paint, and with white spirit (paint thinner) or a proprietary brush cleaner for oil-based (gloss) paint. Soak hardened paint in paint remover overnight, then wash out with hot soapy water.

Household paintbrushes are available in a wide variety of sizes. The bristle quality and length tend to vary, and it is best to choose longer bristles. These brushes are used for all basic painting, edging and varnishing.

Stippling brushes have large blocks of stiff bristles attached to an angled handle. They are used for making fine pinpoint marks. Stippling brushes are available in a variety of sizes. You can use a stiff-bristled masonry brush as an alternative.

Swordliner brushes are long, soft brushes used for marbling effects.

graining brush

softener (blending) brush

dragging brush

swordliner brush

household brush

stippling brush

ROLLERS AND SPONGES

Many types of specialist roller are used in decorating. Specific covers are suitable for different surfaces and you can buy rollers designed for particular patterns. A radiator roller has a long handle for reaching into tight spots. Use small craft and mini-rollers for applying paint in techniques such as stamping. Paint pads can also be useful for clean, flat painting and precise edges, and are made from plastic foam with a short-haired pile inserted into an applicator or handle.

A selection of natural and synthetic sponges is essential for numerous overall decorating techniques, as are lint-free cloths and rags. Each makes its own individual marks.

Mini-rollers have a cover made from dense foam or pile. Available in several widths, they are used for painting narrow stripes or coating stamps.

Masonry rollers are generally 23cm (9in) wide and have a long pile. Use them for covering rough-textured surfaces and for roller fidgeting.

Sheepskin rollers are used for basic quick coverage of flat paint. They are usually available in 18cm (7in) and 23cm (9in) widths.

Use a sponge roller as a cheaper alternative to a sheepskin one. Sponge rollers are also available in 18cm (7in) and 23cm (9in) widths.

Natural sponges are mostly used for sponging. Synthetic sponges make a more obvious mark than natural sponges, so use natural examples for producing tight, fine marks and to create marbled effects.

A chamois, made from real leather, can be scrunched into a ball for ragging. Or use a special ragging chamois, made from strips bound together.

LEFT (clockwise from top left): natural sponge, cloth, pinched-out synthetic sponge, two paint pads, mini-roller, small cellulose sponges, gloss roller, masonry roller, ragging chamois.

SPECIALIST TOOLS

There are many items that will make it easier to plan your decoration. For careful measuring and marking before you start, you may need a spirit (carpenter's) level, long rule, tape measure and pencil. A plumb line, which consists of a small weight suspended on a fine string, is helpful for marking vertical drops. Masking tape is useful for keeping edges straight and covering light switches and sockets.

For certain techniques, special tools are needed. Different shapes of rubber combs will give a variety of woodgrain effects. A heart grainer (graining roller) with its moulded surface will enable you to reproduce the characteristics of a particular wood more accurately. For gilding, a gilder's pad is a useful investment and consists of a soft pad surrounded by a screen of parchment to shield gold leaf from draughts. Craft knives can be bought with double-ended blades that are screwed into the handle and turned or replaced when blunt. Others have a long retractable strip blade that allows you to break off and dispose of the blunt portion. For safety, keep your fingers behind the cutting edge. Never leave the knife within reach of children or where it will be a danger to animals; a piece of cork makes a good protective cap to put on the end of the blade. Craft knives are ideal for cutting out stencils and stamps.

Keep a supply of different grades of abrasive paper, and a sanding block to use with them. A power sander can also save time when tackling larger jobs. If you need to sand an area of floorboards, the best solution is to hire a purpose-built industrial-quality sander.

RIGHT (clockwise from top left): spirit (carpenter's) level, long rule, sanding block, two combs, plumb line, tape measure, heart grainer (graining roller), sanding sponge, craft knife, pencil, selection of abrasive papers (far right).

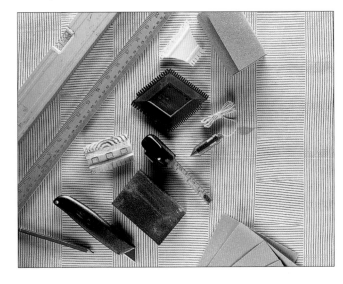

PAINTS

Different paints are suitable for different surfaces and effects, and it is important to choose the right paint for the right surface.

Traditional paints are either water-based or oil-based and generally come in three finishes – matt (flat), satin (mid sheen) and gloss. Most basic wall effects are painted with water-based emulsion (latex) paint since it is easy to apply with a variety of brushes, rollers, sponges and rags. It makes a good base coat, mixes well and can be applied in several layers to build up the desired effect. You can tint white emulsion paint with acrylic paints to make your own colours.

Artists' oil colours are frequently used for faux effects. The rich pigments replicate the colours found in different types of wood, marble and other natural surfaces. Oil paints take longer

to dry than water-based paints, but this can be an advantage if you need to take time in creating a precise effect. They give a more durable finish, but they are a little harder to work with.

Many surfaces benefit from the application of a primer. Primer paints seal and provide a suitable base for paint finishes. They are particularly important if you are working on a porous surface and essential for bare wood. Read the information on the can to make sure you are choosing the correct primer for the specific surface. An undercoat on top of a primer protects the surface further and helps to give a smooth base for the top coat. Oil-based undercoats tend to be used most frequently for painting woodwork.

BELOW: Traditional household paints are available in a tempting array of luscious colours.

PAINT QUALITIES

	BASE	DILUENT	USES	NOTES
Matt emulsion (latex)	water	water, wallpaper paste, acrylic glaze, acrylic varnish; clean with water	basic walls; large choice of colours, flat finish	fast drying, needs varnishing on furniture, marks easily
Silk emulsion (latex)	water	as above	as above; faint sheen	fast drying, more hard-wearing than matt, needs varnishing on furniture
Soft sheen	water	as above	kitchens and bathrooms; mid sheen	fast drying, moisture-resistant, needs varnishing on furniture
Dead flat oil	oil	linseed oil, white spirit (paint thinner), oil glaze, oil varnishes	woodwork; flat/velvet finish	marks easily, not durable
Eggshell	oil	as above	woodwork, furniture; faint sheen	more resistant than above, but still marks
Satin	oil	as above	woodwork, furniture; mid sheen	durable, washable finish
Gloss	oil	as above	woodwork, exterior furniture; high sheen	tough, hard-wearing finish, washable
Primer	oil	not to be diluted; clean with spirits (alcohol)	bare wood	necessary for porous or wood surfaces
Undercoat	oil	not to be diluted; clean with spirits (alcohol)	between the primer and top coat	saves on top coats, choose the right colour
Masonry	water	not to be diluted; clean with water	exterior masonry	limited colours, apply with a suitable roller
Floor	oil	not to be diluted; clean with spirits (alcohol)	floors, light or industrial use	tough, durable, apply with a roller

HOUSEHOLD PAINTS

These are available in a wide range of finishes, from completely matt through varying sheens to high glosses. There is a wealth of colour choice, and in many do-it-yourself stores you can have an exact colour matched and specially mixed for you. Read the instructions on the can before use to check that it is suitable for your surface. When thinning paint, make sure that you are using the correct diluent.

BINDERS AND DILUENTS

Pigment needs a binder so that it will adhere to the surface on which it is painted. As well as the binder in the manufacture of the paint, there are other binders that you can add to modify its consistency and texture. Diluents and solvents are added to thin the paint and to delay the drying time. Glazes also delay drying, and modern products such as acrylic glazes can be used instead of traditional scumble glazes for an easier consistency.

There are many mediums for glazes, such as wallpaper paste, linseed oil, PVA (white) glue and dryers that will change the nature of the paint. Solvents such as white spirit (paint

thinner) can also be used to clean paintbrushes. Make sure you use a diluent or solvent that is suitable for the type of paint you are using.

Regardless of how you employ them, remember that solvents other than water give off toxic fumes and are highly flammable. Treat them with respect and make sure your work area is well ventilated. Never smoke nearby.

Take care when disposing of empty containers and any rags soaked in paint. The latter can ignite spontaneously if exposed to even gentle heat. Do not pour solvent used for cleaning brushes into a drain; take it to a proper disposal site.

BINDERS AND DILUENTS

	BASE	DILUENT	USES	NOTES
PVA (white) glue	water	water	binder for emulsion (latex) washes	makes the mixture more durable
Linseed oil	oil		medium for powder	lengthy drying
Dryers			add to oil paint to speed drying	
Wallpaper paste	water		dilutes emulsion (latex)	retards the drying a little
Acrylic glaze	water	water	as above	retards drying
Scumble glaze	oil	white spirit (paint thinner)	medium to suspend colour pigments	difficult to tint to the right quantity
Methylated spirit (methyl alcohol)	oil		softens dried emulsion (latex)	
White spirit (paint thinner)	oil		paint thinner, brush cleaner	buy in bulk

VARNISHES

U se varnishes to seal and protect the surface of the paint, preserving your decoration. There are specific formulas for interior and exterior use, and they are usually available in matt (flat), satin (mid sheen) or gloss finishes. Modern varnishes have been developed with a polyurethane or acrylic base. Special mediums such as crackle glaze can be used to produce a cracked surface for an antiqued effect. Size acts as a sealant and as a base for gilding.

Varnishes are bought in liquid form or as aerosol sprays. Gloss varnish produces a shiny finish, while matt varnish has a flat look. Make sure you buy the appropriate varnish for interior or exterior use. There are several types of crackle medium on the market, so read the manufacturer's instructions carefully before using one.

ABOVE: Varnishes seal and protect the surface, and add colour to wood.

VARNISHES

	BASE	DILUENT	USES	NOTES
Polyurethane/oil-based	oil	white spirit (paint thinner)	strong varnishes in a range of finishes	tough, durable, slow drying
Polyurethane (aerosol)	oil		flat finish	
Acrylic	water	water	range of finishes	not as durable
Acrylic (aerosol)	water		flat finish	
Tinted varnish	oil	white spirit (paint thinner)	for bare wood, or antiquing paint;	slow drying
	acrylic	water	range of colours	fast drying
Button polish	water	methylated spirit	sealing bare wood	quick drying

PREPARING PAINTED WOODWORK

Modern paints have excellent adhesion and covering power, but to deliver the best performance they must be given a good start by preparing the surface thoroughly.

Wash surfaces that have previously been painted with a solution of strong household detergent or sugar soap (all-purpose cleaner). Rinse them very thoroughly with clean water, and allow them to dry completely before repainting them.

Remove areas of flaking paint with a scraper or putty knife, then either touch in the bare area with more paint or fill it flush with the surrounding paint film by using fine filler (spackle). Sand this smooth when it has hardened.

1 Use fine-grade abrasive paper wrapped around a sanding block to remove "nibs" from the paint surface and key it for repainting.

2 Wash down the surface with detergent or sugar soap (all-purpose cleaner) to remove dirt, grease, finger marks and the dust from sanding it. Rinse with clean water, ensuring that no detergent residue is left, as this will inhibit the new paint film.

3 Use a proprietary tack rag or a clean cloth moistened with white spirit (paint thinner) to remove dust from the recesses of decorative mouldings and other awkward corners. This is most important to ensure a fine finish.

REMOVING OLD PAINT

Stripping is the best option if the paintwork looks in poor condition. It may be deeply chipped or have been badly painted, leaving drips and blobs on the surface. In these cases, it is unlikely that simply applying a new coat of paint will disguise the imperfections on the surface.

You can remove thick layers of old paint with a chemical paint remover in the form of a paste or a liquid stripper that you brush over the paint surface. Wait for the chemicals to react with the paint, then scrape it off with a paint scraper. These chemicals are strong, so read the manufacturer's instructions carefully before applying them and use them properly.

Another way to strip off old paint is to use an electric heat gun. Again, keep safety well in mind and wear protective glasses or goggles to guard your eyes. Too much heat can scorch the wood or crack glass if you are not careful. Put the old scrapings in a metal container as you work and cover surrounding areas, such as the floor, to protect them from accidental damage.

USING LIQUID PAINT STRIPPER

1 Wear rubber gloves and old clothing. Decant the liquid into a glass or plastic container or an old can, then brush it on to the surface. Leave it until the paint film bubbles up.

2 Use a flat scraper or shavehook (triangular scraper) as appropriate to remove the softened paint. Deposit the scrapings safely out of the way in a container.

3 Neutralize the stripper by washing down the surface with water or white spirit (paint thinner), as recommended by the manufacturer. Leave the stripped area to dry.

FILLING DEFECTS AND CRACKS

A perfectly smooth, flat surface is essential for a good paint finish, and if you intend painting a wood or plaster surface, there are likely to be cracks and other minor blemishes that need filling before you can begin painting.

If you have chosen an opaque finish, cracks and small holes in wood can be filled with cellulose filler (spackle). However, if you intend applying a varnish or similar translucent finish, a tinted wood stopper (patcher) would be more appropriate, since it will disguise the damage. Cracks in plaster should be treated with cellulose filler.

Always apply filler so that it is a little proud of the surrounding surface. Then, when it has dried, sand it back to leave a perfectly smooth surface.

FILLING DEFECTS IN WOOD

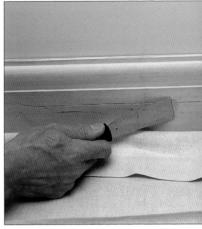

1 Fill splits and dents in wood using filler (spackle) on painted surfaces, and tinted wood stopper (patcher) on new or stripped wood that will be varnished.

2 Use the corner of a putty knife blade, or even a finger, to work the filler into recesses and other awkward-to-reach places. Smooth off excess filler before it dries.

3 When the filler or wood stopper has hardened completely, use abrasive paper wrapped around a sanding block to sand down the repair flush with the surroundings.

FILLING CRACKS IN PLASTER

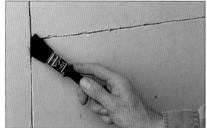

1 Use a putty knife to rake out loose material along the crack, and to undercut the edges so that the filler (spackle) grips well.

2 Brush out dust and debris from the crack, using an old paintbrush. Alternatively, use the crevice nozzle attachment of a vacuum cleaner.

3 Dampen the surrounding plaster with water from a garden spray gun to prevent it from drying out the filler too quickly and causing the repair to crack.

4 Mix up some filler on a plasterer's hawk (mortarboard) or a board offcut to a firm consistency. Alternatively, use ready-mixed filler or wallboard compound.

5 Use a filling knife to press the filler well into the crack, drawing the blade across it and then along it. Aim to leave the repair slightly proud at this stage.

6 When the filler has hardened, use fine-grade abrasive paper wrapped around a sanding block to smooth the repair until it is flush with the surrounding surface.

USING BRUSHES AND ROLLERS

Paint is applied using brushes, rollers or paint pads. Brushes are available in a range of widths, so choose one that is suitable for the surface you are painting – for instance, use a narrow brush for the glazing bars of a window. For large areas, use a wide brush, or a roller for fast coverage.

If you wish to paint with a previously used brush that has not been kept covered, wash it well first to remove any bits and pieces. Leave it to dry before using it. Check that the ferrule of the brush, which secures the bristles, is securely fixed to the handle and clean off any traces of rust with wire (steel) wool or abrasive paper.

Rollers are excellent for dealing with large flat areas. Choose a suitable sleeve depending on whether you are painting on smooth plaster or a textured surface. You may also need to use a brush in corners where the roller will not fit.

USING A BRUSH

1 Use small or medium brushes by placing your fingers on one side of the ferrule and your thumb on the other. This gives you better control.

2 Wide brushes will be heavy, particularly when loaded with paint, so hold them by the handle, otherwise your hand will quickly become tired.

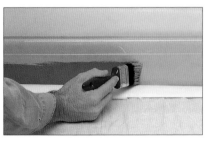

3 Dip only a third of the bristles into the paint. Use long sweeping strokes, working in the direction of the grain, until the paint is used. Then reload with paint and apply it to the next section.

4 Blend the two sections together with short, light strokes. Paint edges and corners by letting the brush run off the edge and repeating the process on the opposite edge.

USING A ROLLER

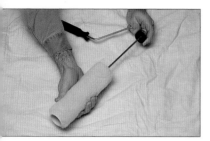

1 Select a sleeve with the required fibre type and pile length, and slide it on to the sprung metal cage until it meets the stop next to the handle.

2 Decant some paint (previously strained if from an old can) into the roller tray until the paint level just laps up the sloping section.

3 Brush a band of paint about 50mm (2in) wide into wall/ceiling angles, around doors and windows, and above skirtings (baseboards). Brush out the edge so that it does not form a seam.

4 Load the roller sleeve with paint by running it down the sloping section into the paint. Then roll it up and down the slope to remove the excess. Make sure the tray cannot be upset accidentally.

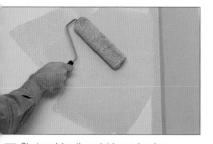

5 Start applying the paint in overlapping diagonal strokes to ensure complete coverage. Continue until the sleeve runs dry. Do not "drive" the roller too quickly, as it may cause splashes.

6 Reload the sleeve and tackle the next section in the same way. Finish off by blending the areas together, working parallel to corners and edges.

BASIC FINISHES

The techniques demonstrated in this section show you how to achieve a variety of traditional paint effects, most of which can be used to obtain an all-over impact. In the main, they are suitable for decorating large surface areas, such as walls, quickly and with ease. Several, such as distressing and lacquering, are ideal for putting your own personal stamp on furniture, while others – for example, applying crackle glaze – will enable you to transform small items and home accessories into something decorative and special. Spend some time practising the various techniques on pieces of scrap board until you are happy that you can achieve exactly the effect you want.

COLOURWASHING

You can dilute emulsion (latex) paint with water, wallpaper paste and emulsion glaze to make a mixture known as a wash. The effect varies depending on the consistency of the paint mixture and the method of applying the colour, but it is usually done with a broad brush.

In this instance, a large paintbrush has been used, but you could also employ a synthetic sponge to achieve a different effect.

Materials

emulsion (latex) paint	paint kettle
wallpaper paste	large paintbrush

COLOUR EFFECTS

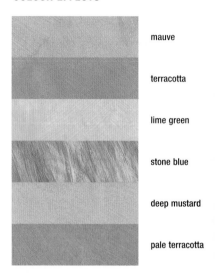

mauve

terracotta

lime green

stone blue

deep mustard

pale terracotta

1 Using a paint kettle, mix 50 per cent emulsion (latex) paint with 50 per cent wallpaper paste (premixed to a thin solution). Using at least a 10cm (4in) brush (up to 15cm/6in), dip the tip into the mixture and wipe off the excess on the side of the kettle. Add the first dashes on to the wall, well spaced.

2 Without adding more paint, brush out these dashes in random directions, using broad sweeping strokes. Continue working along the wall, adding a little more paint as you go and using quite a dry brush to blend the seams between areas of paint.

COLOURWASHING LAYERS

This is done in the same way as colourwashing one layer, but once the first layer is dry a second colour is applied on top. This layering will soften the overall effect of the brush or sponge marks. Experiment with different colour variations (contrasting and complementary) and layering combinations until you have achieved the effect you want, using a large piece of board as your "canvas".

Materials

emulsion (latex) paint in two colours

wallpaper paste

paint kettle

large paintbrush

COLOUR EFFECTS

camel under cream

purple under mauve

jade green under pale green

blue under cream

terracotta under yellow

red under pale yellow

1 Mix the paint in a paint kettle, using 50 per cent emulsion (latex) paint and 50 per cent wallpaper paste (premixed to a thin solution). Apply the paint to the wall with random strokes, varying the direction as you go. Continue until you have covered the whole surface.

2 When the first layer has been allowed to dry completely, repeat step 1, using a second colour of paint. Add more paint and soften the joins between areas. The overall colourwash effect will be much softer than when applying only one colour.

SPONGING

Large areas can be covered quickly and easily using the simple technique of sponging, perfect for beginners. Varied effects can be made by using either a synthetic sponge or a natural sponge. A natural sponge will produce smaller, finer marks, while heavier marks can be created with a synthetic sponge. Pinching out small chunks will avoid straight edges. You may find edges and corners are a bit tricky with a large sponge, so use a smaller piece of sponge for these.

Materials

emulsion (latex) paint   natural sponge

COLOUR EFFECTS

cream over terracotta

blue over lilac

mustard over white

grey over white

lime green over white

lilac over mauve

1 Pour the paint into a shallow container and dip the sponge into it; scrape off the excess paint on the edge of the container, ensuring that there are no blobs left on the sponge. Lightly dab the paint on to the surface, varying the angle of application to prevent a uniform appearance.

2 Add more paint to the wall, continuing to work over the surface until you have covered it completely. If necessary, fill in any gaps and make sure that the overall pattern is of similar "weight" – not too heavy in some areas or too light in others.

SPONGING LAYERS

The technique is the same as for sponging one layer, but the overall effect is deepened by the addition of one or more other colours. After the first has been applied and allowed to dry, you can proceed with the second, taking care not to put on too much paint, otherwise you will obliterate the colour below. Experiment with colour combinations, and perhaps try using a natural sponge for one layer and a synthetic sponge for another.

Materials

emulsion (latex) paint   natural sponge
  in two colours

COLOUR EFFECTS

turquoise
and lime green

pale terracotta
and yellow

purple
and grey

cornflower blue
and grey

orange, red
and yellow

pale green, jade
and grey

1 Apply a single layer by dipping the sponge into the paint, then scrape off the excess and dab on to the wall for an even pattern. Making the pattern even is not quite so important when applying two colours because the second layer will soften the effect. Allow the surface to dry completely.

2 Make sure the sponge is completely clean and dry. Dip it into the second colour paint, scraping off the excess as before and dabbing on to the surface. Do not apply too much paint, however, as you must make sure the first colour isn't totally covered.

DRAGGING

A special dragging brush is often used to achieve this effect, but it can also be done with a household paintbrush or even the end of a sponge. The technique is very simple – the brush is pulled down over wet paint in a clean line to produce a striped effect. These lines must be unbroken, so painting a full-height room may prove extremely difficult. To overcome this, a horizontal band can be added to break up the height of the room.

Materials

pencil	paint kettle
rule	large paintbrush
emulsion (latex) paint	dragging brush
wallpaper paste	damp cloth

1 Draw a horizontal baseline across the wall at dado (chair rail) level. Mix emulsion (latex) paint with 50 per cent wallpaper paste (premixed to a thin solution) in a paint kettle and brush on in a lengthways band, slightly overlapping the baseline. Work on one small section at a time, about 15–25cm (6–10in) wide.

COLOUR EFFECTS

terracotta

brown

stone blue

yellow

biscuit

powder blue

4 Drag straight over the join between the two areas of paint and carry on dragging. Continue in this way from one end of the wall to the other.

2 Dampen the dragging brush with the wash before use, as initially it will take off too much paint if used dry. Then take the brush in one hand and flatten the bristles out with your other hand. Pull the brush down in as straight a motion as possible. This will create deep groove lines in the paint mixture.

3 Brush on another band of paint mixture, adjacent to the last one and overlapping it slightly. Do not cover too large an area at a time, otherwise the paint may become unworkable as it begins to dry.

5 Once this top section has been done, take a damp cloth and, pulling along the pencil line, remove the excess paint.

6 Drag in a horizontal motion across the bottom of the baseline, creating subtle stripes in a different direction.

STIPPLING

A delicate and subtle finish can be achieved by stippling. The technique consists of making fine, pinpoint marks over a wash of emulsion (latex) paint, and it creates a soft, mottled effect. However, it can be quite tiring to do, as the brush has to be dabbed over the surface many times, using firm, even pressure. Two people can speed up the process, one person applying the paint and the other stippling the surface.

Materials

emulsion (latex) paint	household paintbrush
paint kettle	stippling brush
wallpaper paste	

COLOUR EFFECTS

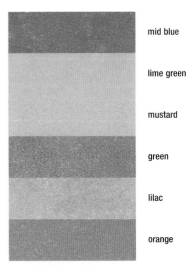

mid blue

lime green

mustard

green

lilac

orange

1 Mix a wash of 50 per cent emulsion (latex) paint and 50 per cent wallpaper paste, premixed to a thin solution, in a paint kettle. Brush on a thin, even coat of the mixture, covering an area of about 0.2 sq m (2 sq ft).

2 Take the stippling brush and dab over the surface with the tips of the bristles until the effect is even all over. Continue stippling the surface until there are no obvious joins (seams) and the whole effect looks soft and even.

ROLLER FIDGETING

This is a quick and simple technique and consists of pouring two undiluted emulsion (latex) paint colours into a roller tray, one at each side. You will find that the two paints will sit quite happily together and do not instantly mix. Then, a long-pile masonry roller is skimmed over the surface of these colours until a good thick coat is applied. This is rollered on to the wall at varying angles.

Materials

paint tray	long-pile masonry roller
emulsion (latex) paint in two colours	2.5cm (1in) household paintbrush

COLOUR EFFECTS

red and camel

mid blue and grey

grey and cream

yellow and cream

pale mauve and dark mauve

mid blue and green

1 Pour two colours, one on each side of the pool of the roller tray. Apply a thick coat from here on to the roller so that it will create a two-tone effect. Apply the roller to the wall at varying angles, using short strokes.

2 Continue without applying more paint to the roller until the colours are slightly softened together. Keep the angles as random as possible. Go over the whole effect with the roller to soften it. Add more paint when starting another area.

RAGGING

There are two methods of ragging – ragging on and ragging off – and both techniques are as simple as they sound. With ragging on, you dab the rag into the paint, then dab on to the surface. The technique is similar to sponging, but leaves a sharper effect. The effect will vary depending whether you use a similar colour to the base or a strongly contrasting one. Make sure that the ragging is applied evenly.

Materials

emulsion (latex) paint	roller tray
wallpaper paste	large paintbrush
paint kettle	chamois

Ragging off produces a stronger effect, like crumpled fabric. You brush paint on to the surface, then use a rag to remove some of the paint, leaving a ragged print. The recommended "rag" to use is a chamois, as it creates a definite print, although you can use most types of cloth for a particular effect.

When using either of the techniques, it is important to apply the rag to the wall with firm, but gentle, pressure. When you remove it, lift it cleanly from the surface without any vertical or sideways movement that might smear the paint and spoil the finished effect. The chamois leather should be squeezed out periodically.

RAGGING ON

1 Mix 50 per cent emulsion (latex) paint with 50 per cent wallpaper paste in a paint kettle. Pour into a roller tray. Scrunch up a chamois, dip it into the paint and dab off the excess, then dab the "rag" on to the wall.

2 Continue re-scrunching the chamois and dipping it into the paint as before, then dabbing it on to the wall in a random manner. Carry on in this way until the surface has been covered evenly and completely.

RAGGING OFF

1 Mix 50 per cent emulsion (latex) and 50 per cent wallpaper paste as before. Brush the wash over a large area.

2 Take a chamois, scrunch it up and dab on to the wall to remove small areas of paint. Vary the angle with each dab.

COLOUR EFFECTS

mid blue

deep mauve

biscuit

grey

pale mauve

terracotta

3 Continue working over the surface until the entire effect is even. If you find you are taking off too much paint, apply more immediately with a brush, then dab the chamois over the surface in the same manner as before.

DISTRESSING

This is a way of ageing paint to create chips and scratches that would occur naturally on a painted piece of furniture over a matter of time. The method shown here employs petroleum jelly and candle wax, but you can use just one or the other. This creates a barrier between the surface and the paint, so once the paint is dry it can be lifted away in certain areas where the medium has been applied.

Materials

petroleum jelly	paint scraper
artists' paintbrush	soapy water
emulsion (latex) paint	wax candle
household paintbrush	varnish

1 Using an artists' paintbrush, load it with petroleum jelly and apply long blobs in the direction of the grain of wood over a suitably coloured base coat. Even if the surface is not wooden, rub in a lengthways direction.

COLOUR EFFECTS

blue over
yellow
over wood

mauve over
blue over wood

green over
blue over wood

orange over
yellow
over wood

purple over
red over wood

blue over
burnt orange
over wood

4 Wash down thoroughly with soapy water, as the paint that is sitting on top of the petroleum jelly will not actually dry and you will not be able to totally remove the petroleum jelly surface by using the scraper alone.

2 Carefully paint the surface, making sure it is covered completely, but ensuring that the petroleum jelly is not dragged about too much, since it will spread readily under the action of the paintbrush. Allow the paint to dry thoroughly.

3 Once the paint has dried completely, carefully go over the surface with a paint scraper. This will lift off the areas of paint where the petroleum jelly has prevented contact between the top coat and base coat.

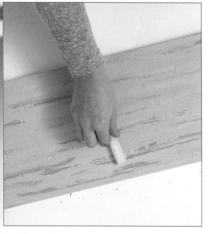

5 Once dry, rub over with a wax candle and then paint again, using a contrasting colour. (You could use another layer of petroleum jelly, following the same procedure as before, but the finished effect would not look as subtle.)

6 When the paint is dry, go over the surface once more with a paint scraper to lift off the areas over the candle wax. Wipe down to remove all the flakes of paint, then apply a coat of varnish to protect the surface.

WOOD WASHING

You can stain wood with a colour while allowing the beauty of the grain to show through, using wood washing (wood staining). The wood must be bare, either new or stripped of all traces of varnish, wax or previous paint. Depending on the product used, the surface may or may not need varnishing – read the manufacturer's instructions. Usually a matt (flat) finish looks appropriate for this technique.

Materials

specialist wood wash (wood stain)	household paintbrush
paint kettle	cloth

COLOUR EFFECTS

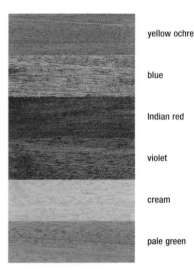

yellow ochre

blue

Indian red

violet

cream

pale green

1 Pour the premixed wash (stain) into a paint kettle. Then brush the wash evenly on to the wood, working in the direction of the grain. Keep a "wet" edge and do not overlap areas.

2 While wet, wipe off the excess with a cloth. This will even the effect and expose slightly more of the grain. Then leave to dry before varnishing if required.

CRACKLE GLAZE

This technique reproduces the effect of old, crackled paint, but it can only work if you use a special crackle-glaze medium. A base coat is applied first, and when dry, a layer of crackle glaze is added. This is followed by a top coat of paint, which will not be able to grip the base coat while drying and subsequently will shrink and crack to produce a crackled effect. You can achieve some striking colour combinations with this technique.

Materials

emulsion (latex) paint in two colours	household paintbrush crackle-glaze medium

COLOUR EFFECTS

mustard over red

navy over pale blue

mid blue over yellow

turquoise over lime green

lilac over purple

yellow over red

1 Apply a coat of base colour and leave to dry thoroughly. Then apply a second coat of base colour and allow to dry again. Apply a good solid coat of crackle-glaze medium. The timing for applying the various coats will vary according to the manufacturer, so follow the instructions given on the container.

2 Apply the top coat. Generally, the thicker the top coat of paint, the larger the cracks in the final effect. Make sure the top coat contrasts greatly with the one underneath so that the cracks are obvious. Do not overbrush when applying the top coat, as the effect occurs quite quickly and you could spoil it.

LACQUERING

This creates a totally smooth, flat and highly polished paint finish that reflects great depth of colour. The traditional method of lacquering, as perfected by Asian craftsmen, is very time-consuming and consists of applying at least 16 layers of paint. A simulated version is shown here, using rich colours finished with a high gloss varnish. Aerosol spray paints are used for the last layers because they will create the smoothest surface possible.

Materials

fine-grade abrasive paper	household paintbrush
	spray gloss enamel
gloss paint	spray gloss varnish

COLOUR EFFECTS

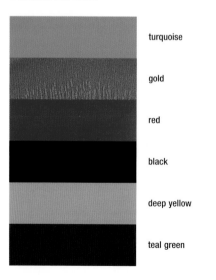

turquoise

gold

red

black

deep yellow

teal green

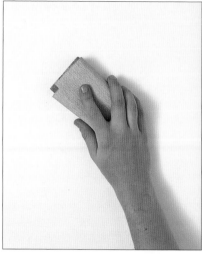

1 Sand the surface thoroughly until totally smooth. Then wipe clean the surface, making sure that it is completely free of dust.

4 Build up the thickness of the paint film by applying a second brushed-on base coat. Leave this to dry thoroughly, then sand the surface lightly.

2 Apply a base coat of high-gloss paint with a brush, keeping the coverage as even as possible. Leave it to dry thoroughly.

3 Sand the surface with fine-grade abrasive paper wrapped around a sanding block to ensure total smoothness.

5 Spray on a gloss enamel in the same colour as the base coat, keeping the coverage even, and taking care not to spray on too much and cause runs. Again leave to dry thoroughly.

6 Finally, spray a clear gloss varnish over the surface, taking care to avoid runs. This will not only protect the paint, but also provide a smooth lacquer-style finish.

PATTERNED EFFECTS

There is a long tradition of using both simple and complex patterns as forms of decoration, but in the main these have been provided by wallpaper, which is a quick and convenient way of doing the job. However, using paint to make patterns allows you to create something quite unique. There are many ways of applying pattern as a decoration, whether freehand or using a template. With stencilling and stamping, you can add an individual touch to your schemes by choosing designs from a wealth that are available commercially or by drawing, cutting, and using your own stencils and stamps. Classic lines and stripes never seem to go out of fashion, and grid patterns are a fun way of combining colours.

STENCILLING

The decorative possibilities of stencilling are endless, so it is not surprising that it is one of the most popular of paint effects. It is an ideal way to create an interesting border or all-over pattern using motifs that relate to the theme of your room. Stencilling also enables you to co-ordinate furnishings and accessories by picking out details in similar or contrasting colours. Or you can use the patterns and colours of your stencilling as a starting point for the style and colours of your home. The fleur-de-lis and rose design shown here is typical of what can be achieved.

Materials

household sponge	masking tape
emulsion (latex) paint	spray adhesive
in three colours	tracing paper
rule	stencil card or acetate
spirit (carpenter's)	two motif stencils
level	stencil brush and fine
pencil	lining brush

1 Using a large sponge, rub the first emulsion (latex) colour on the wall. Leave to dry. Repeat using a second colour to cover the base. Using a rule and spirit (carpenter's) level, draw a line at dado (chair rail) height and place masking tape above it. Sponge your third colour below this.

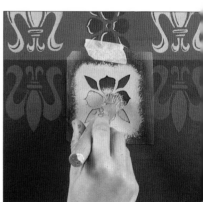

4 When you have completed a line of motifs above the dividing line, make sure that the paint on the faces of the stencils is completely dry (or cut new ones), then flip the stencils over and position them as mirror images below the original motifs. Stencil the roses in the base colour and the fleur-de-lis in the second colour.

2 If necessary, cut stencils from stencil card or acetate. Secure the rose stencil above the dividing line and stencil in your third colour with a stencil brush. When dry, position the fleur-de-lis stencil next to the first and paint in the colour of the base coat. Alternate stencils around the room.

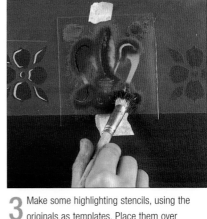

3 Make some highlighting stencils, using the originals as templates. Place them over the painted motifs and, with a stencil brush, add highlights in the base colour to the first stencilled design, and highlights in the third colour to the second design.

5 Allow the paint to dry, then go back and add highlights to the motifs as before, using base colour on the fleur-de-lis and the third colour on the roses. Again, make sure that there is no wet paint on the faces of the flipped stencils, since this could be transferred to the wall and spoil the overall effect.

6 Using a fine lining brush and the base colour paint, paint a narrow line where the two different colours on the wall meet. If you do not have the confidence to do this freehand, position two lines of masking tape on the wall, leaving a small gap between them. When the line of paint is dry, carefully remove the masking tape.

STAMPING

Like stencilling, stamping allows you to create your own decorative motifs. It is easy and inexpensive to cut out shapes in relief from high-density sponge and to use them to apply paint. However, you can also achieve quite sophisticated effects with this simple technique, and the steps here show how to add a special touch to a room by stamping panels with gold leaf. This is achieved by stamping the wall with gold size first, then rubbing on gold leaf, which will adhere to the tacky surface.

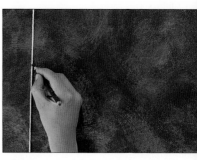

1 Fold a 30cm (12in) square piece of card in half, cut an arc from corner to corner and unfold to create a symmetrical arch template.

Materials

card (card stock)	household sponge
rule	plumb line
pencil	tape measure
scissors	small paint roller
high-density sponge	gold size
craft knife	Dutch Metal
emulsion (latex) paint	(simulated gold leaf)
in jade green and	soft brush
purple	

4 Using a plumb line as a guide, and beginning 23cm (9in) from a corner, mark a vertical line up the wall to a height of 1.8m (6ft). Use the plumb line to draw vertical lines every 60cm (2ft).

7 When the size is tacky, apply Dutch gold leaf to it by rubbing over the backing paper with a soft brush. Peel the backing away.

2 Transfer a design on to a piece of high-density sponge. Using a craft knife, cut away excess sponge from around the shape.

3 Apply jade green emulsion (latex) paint to the wall using a sponge and working in a circular motion. Allow the paint to dry.

5 Measure 15cm (6in) to each side of each line and draw two more vertical lines to mark the edges of the panels. Place the template at the top of each panel and draw in the curves.

6 Load the stamp with gold size and apply it to the areas within the outlined panels, beginning at the centre top and working down in horizontal lines. Reload the stamp as necessary.

8 Once the panel has been gilded completely, go over it with a soft brush to remove any excess gold leaf.

9 Using the centre of the stamp, fill in the spaces between the gold motifs with purple emulsion paint.

STRIPES

A classic design for decorating schemes, stripes are extremely versatile, as you can vary their width for any number of effects. If you are aiming for a symmetrical, formal look, it is important to measure out the available space accurately first so that you can be sure the stripes will fit. It is helpful to draw out the design in a small scale on a piece of paper to work out the correct balance.

Materials

emulsion (latex) paint in two colours	pencil
paint roller	masking tape
paint tray	acrylic scumble
paintbrushes	nylon stocking
	cardboard

1 Paint the walls. Mark the centre of the most important wall with a pencil. Make marks 7.5cm (3in) on each side of this, then every 15cm (6in). Continue around the room until the marks meet at the least noticeable corner.

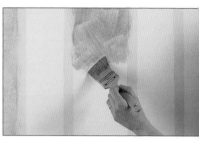

4 Dilute some of the second colour with about 25 per cent water and 25 per cent acrylic scumble. Complete each stripe in two or three stages, blending the joins to achieve an even result.

7 Working on one stripe at a time, place masking tape between the top corners and the mark. Brush on the second colour, then dab the stocking over the wet paint. Leave to dry.

2 Hang a short length of plumb line from one of the marks, and mark with a dot where it rests. Then, hang the plumb line from this dot and mark where it rests. Continue down the wall. Repeat for each mark below the picture rail.

3 Starting in the centre of the wall, place strips of masking tape on alternate sides of the marked rows of dots to give 15cm (6in) wide stripes. Repeat until you have taped all the walls.

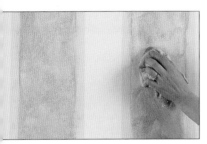

5 Dab the wet paint lightly with the stocking to smooth out the brush marks. Complete all the stripes, peel off the masking tape and leave the paint to dry.

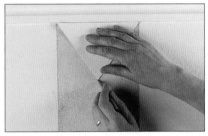

6 From a piece of cardboard, cut a triangle with a 15cm (6in) base and measuring 10cm (4in) from base to tip. Use this to mark the centre of each stripe.

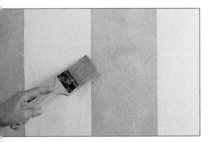

8 Dilute some of the second colour paint with 20 parts water to one part paint. Brush this over the wall, working in all directions to give a hint of colour to the first colour stripes.

9 Add a little paint to the remaining diluted mixture to strengthen the colour. Using a paint guard or strip of card to protect the painted wall, brush the paint on to the picture rail.

PRINTED TILES

This is an inexpensive and clever way to create a tiled effect with simple painted squares. Fine tape separates the tiles and is removed when the effect is finished to give the illusion of grouting. Leave some of the squares plain, but add extra effects to others by sponging them or dabbing them with a nylon stocking. Experiment with different colours to create your own design, or leave some of the squares white as a contrast. You could also experiment with mosaic patterns by measuring and masking much smaller squares with fine lining tape before applying the second colour. You need not restrict yourself to creating squares either; you could try oblongs, triangles or diamonds, or perhaps even combinations of these shapes.

1 Paint the wall in white, using a paint roller to achieve an even texture. Decide on the width of your "tiled" panel. Mark the wall 45cm (18in) above your work surface and in the centre of the width measurement.

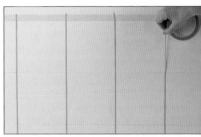

4 Place fine masking tape over the lines in both directions. Smooth the tape into place with your fingers, pressing it down well to ensure that paint does not seep underneath it.

Materials

emulsion (latex) paint in white and a second colour	standard, fine and low-tack masking tape
paint roller	sponge
paint tray	kitchen paper (paper towels)
paintbrush	nylon stocking
rule	eraser
pencil	
spirit (carpenter's) level	

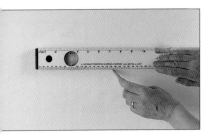

2 Draw a horizontal line across the wall at this height, using a spirit (carpenter's) level to make sure that it is straight and level. Apply a strip of standard masking tape to the wall above the line, making sure that it butts up to it accurately.

3 Mark dots along the tape at 15cm (6in) intervals on each side of the centre mark. Use the spirit level to draw vertical lines down the wall. Mark along the vertical lines at 15cm (6in) intervals and connect them with horizontal lines.

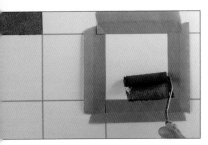

5 Place low-tack masking tape around one square. Pour the second colour into the paint tray and add 25 per cent water. Roll an even coat over the square. Repeat for all plain squares.

6 Mask off a square to be sponged. Dampen the sponge, dip it into the second colour and dab the excess on to kitchen paper (paper towels). Sponge the square. Repeat for other squares.

7 Mask off a square to be dabbed with the nylon stocking. Apply the paint with a brush, then use the stocking to blend it. Repeat for all the squares needing this effect.

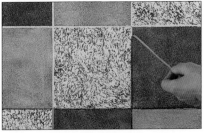

8 Allow the paint to dry partially, then remove the tape while it is still soft. When the paint is completely dry, clean off all the pencil marks with an eraser.

FAUX FINISHES

Techniques that reproduce the look of a particular surface or material are often very challenging, but they can be great fun too, and when done correctly they can produce very realistic and satisfying results. The following pages will show you how to achieve a number of wood and stone finishes that will allow you to create imaginative decorative effects throughout your home. Artists' oil colours are used, since their lengthy drying periods allow more time to work on the effect, and their colours are intense and translucent. Another interesting effect is the trompe l'oeil decoration, in which a picture is painted to deceive the eye into thinking that a flat surface is, in fact, three-dimensional.

PINE

Woodgraining and wood effects can seem difficult and daunting to the beginner, but the right choice of colours and suitable base coats can be half the battle. The only specialist tools used are a heart grainer (graining roller) and comb, which are necessary as the patterns they create cannot be imitated in any other way. Both are relatively simple to use with a little practice and create convincing effects.

Look at pieces of real wood so that you can learn to replicate the grain accurately. Pine is readily available and you can use a pine effect surface in many locations throughout your home.

Materials

satinwood paint in pale yellow	white spirit (paint thinner)
household paintbrush	heart grainer
paint kettle	(graining roller)
artists' oil colour paint in yellow ochre and burnt umber	comb
	large paintbrush
	varnish

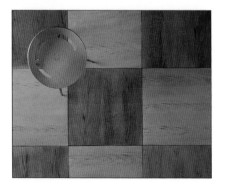

1 Prepare the surface to be woodgrained in the normal manner. Brush on two coats of pale yellow satinwood paint, allowing each coat to dry thoroughly before proceeding.

4 Following the direction of the dragging, pull the heart grainer (graining roller) down gently, rocking it as you work, to create the effect. Butt one line straight over the other.

2 Mix yellow ochre artists' oil colour paint with a tiny amount of burnt umber to dirty the colour slightly. Then mix with white spirit (paint thinner) to create a thick cream, and brush over the surface.

3 Drag the brush in a lengthways direction over the wet paint. This will allow streaks of the base colour to show through, which is the basis for the woodgrain effect.

5 Use the comb to make graduated cone shapes in random positions across the surface between the heart graining, slightly overlapping it in some areas.

6 Soften the surface while wet with a large dry brush, applying only light pressure and brushing in the direction of the effect. Varnish the finish when dry.

OAK

Perhaps nothing speaks more of a traditional style than solid oak wood furniture or panelling. Here is a way of disguising inexpensive white wood or modern pine and giving it the look of dark oak. If you are painting bare wood, remember to give it a coat of primer before starting the paint effect. This technique requires a heart grainer (graining roller) and a comb to re-create the details of the woodgrain, both of which can be bought from most good craft shops and specialist decorating shops.

Materials

gloss or satin paint in beige	paint kettle
paintbrush	graduated comb
artists' oil colour paint in burnt umber	fine graduated comb
	heart grainer (graining roller)
white spirit (paint thinner)	cloth
	large paintbrush
	varnish

1 Prepare the surface to be woodgrained in the normal manner. Apply two coats of beige for the base coat in either gloss or satin finish, allowing each to dry thoroughly.

4 Use a heart grainer (graining roller) to start creating the detailed figuring of the grain. Do this by pulling the tool down gently over the surface with a slight rocking motion, to create the hearts with random spacings. Butt one line straight over the other as you go.

2 Mix burnt umber artists' oil colour paint with white spirit (paint thinner) in a small paint kettle until it is the consistency of thick cream. Brush on and drag in a lengthways direction.

3 Using a graduated comb, pull down on the surface. Do not work in totally straight lines, but make them curve slightly, butting one up against the other.

5 When you are satisfied with the effect that the heart graining produces, take the fine graduated comb and go over all the previous combing. As the work progresses, you will begin to see the finish take on the appearance of genuine oak.

6 Wrap a piece of clean, lint-free cloth around the comb and dab it on to the surface in a random manner to create the angled grain, pressing it into the wet paint. Then soften the overall effect by going over the entire surface with a large dry brush. Varnish when dry.

MAHOGANY

This beautiful hardwood has a rich, warm colour that seems to suit most styles of home, whether traditional or modern. It was extremely popular during the Victorian era when it was complemented by deep-toned furnishings and fabrics. These days it is not ecologically desirable to use mahogany, and it is also hard to come by and expensive, so all the more reason to paint some for yourself. Practise on sample pieces first, then progress to larger furniture when you have more confidence in the technique.

Materials

satin or gloss paint in dusky pink	white spirit (paint thinner)
artists' oil colour paint in burnt sienna, crimson and burnt umber	paint kettles
	paintbrushes in different sizes
	varnish

1 Apply two coats of dusky pink and leave to dry. Tint burnt sienna oil paint with crimson, adding white spirit (paint thinner) to make a thick creamy consistency. Brush on in long strips. Thin burnt umber to a thick cream. Fill gaps with long strips.

2 Stipple the surface gently with a dry paintbrush to soften the overall effect.

3 Starting at the bottom, with a 10cm (4in) paintbrush held almost parallel to the surface, drag through the wet paint in elongated arcs. Use the burnt umber area as the middle section. Before completely dry, soften in one direction using a large dry brush. Varnish when dry.

BEECH

In recent years, beech has become popular for both furniture and home accessories such as trays, and mirror and picture frames. It is a light-coloured, straight-grained wood, and its close patterning gives it a look of solidity. Its soft, warm colour and generally matt finish adds a quiet, but modern, tone to a room as well as helping to lighten it up. Like oak, beech is sometimes given a limed effect, so if this is what you require allow more of the base coat to show through when painting.

Materials

satinwood paint in white	white spirit (paint thinner)
household paintbrush	heart grainer (graining roller)
paint kettle	fine graduated comb
artists' oil colour paint in Naples yellow and white	narrow comb
	varnish

1 Apply two coats of white satinwood and leave to dry. Mix the yellow and white oils with white spirit (paint thinner) until a thick cream; brush on the surface. Drag in a lengthways direction.

2 Use a heart grainer (graining roller) to start graining, pulling it down gently and rocking it slightly, working in spaced lines. Do not butt them together. Use a graduated comb in the same direction to fill in between the heart graining.

3 Again, working in the same direction, soften the effect with a large dry brush. Now take a narrow comb and go over the entire surface in the same direction to add detail. Varnish when dry.

MARBLING

There are many specialist techniques for achieving a marble effect, but here is a very simple method. Types of marble vary greatly in colour and pattern, and it may be a good idea to use a piece of real marble as a reference source. Aim for a general effect of marbled patterning that is subtle in colour, with most of the veining softened to create depth.

Try colour variations of crimson and ultramarine; raw sienna and black; Indian red, yellow ochre and black; raw sienna, yellow ochre and Prussian blue; or Prussian blue and ultramarine.

Materials

satinwood paint in white	small paint kettles
household paintbrush	white spirit (paint thinner)
artists' oil colour paint in ultramarine and yellow ochre	stippling brush
	swordliner brush
	gloss varnish

1 Paint a base coat of white satinwood paint on to the surface and leave to dry. Squeeze a long blob of ultramarine artists' oil colour paint into a paint kettle and add some white spirit (paint thinner) to form a thick cream. Brush on patches of this.

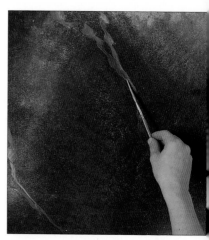

4 Dip a swordliner brush into white spirit and drag it through the wet surface, applying no pressure, but just letting the brush stroke the surface of the paint. Slightly angle the bristles while you pull the brush down.

2 Squeeze some yellow ochre artists' oil colour paint into a second paint kettle and dilute it with white spirit until it is the consistency of thick cream. Fill in the patches where the blue has not been painted with this mixture.

3 While the oil colours are still wet, take a stippling brush and work over the entire surface, blending them gently together. The idea is to make one colour fade gradually into the next without any hard lines.

5 Dip the brush back into the white spirit for each line. The white spirit will finally separate the oil glaze surface. Make sure there are not too many lines and only add the odd fork – the less complicated the pattern, the better the effect will be.

6 Dip the swordliner into the dark blue glaze remaining from step 1 and draw down the side of each painted line with a very fine line. When you are happy with the effect, allow the paint to dry completely, then coat with gloss varnish.

TROMPE L'OEIL SKY

This lovely effect is suitable for any room in which you wish to create a sense of calm and imagine yourself floating away among the clouds. Draw the outline shapes of the clouds lightly on the walls first, but do not feel that you have to follow them rigidly. As you work, you may feel the need to change them, so allow yourself the freedom to paint loose shapes with merging edges to achieve a realistic appearance. Practise on a piece of scrap board first until you are happy with your technique. Adding wallpaper paste to the paint gives texture and depth to the effect.

Materials

emulsion (latex) paint in white and sky blue	pencil
	silk finish emulsion paint in white
household paintbrush	wallpaper paste
sponge	paint kettle

1 Apply two coats of white emulsion (latex) as a base coat, allowing to dry between coats. Dip a sponge into sky blue emulsion paint and rub over the whole surface in a circular motion, leaving a mottled effect. Leave to dry.

4 Dilute white emulsion paint with 50 per cent wallpaper paste and stipple this on to the surface, starting along the top edge of the pencil line. Continue downwards without applying any more paint to the brush; this will gradate the colour.

2 Apply a second coat of sky blue to the wall, using a sponge in the same manner as in step 1. This second coat will leave the whole effect looking almost solid, but with a slightly mottled appearance. Allow to dry.

3 When the blue paint is completely dry, go over the wall with a soft pencil, outlining rough cloud shapes to act as a guide for painting. You need not be too fussy when doing this, since you may change your mind when painting.

5 Build up the depth of the clouds in layers, allowing each to dry before applying the next. Go over the first layer along the top side and then stipple downwards as before. This will strengthen the overall effect.

6 Finally, add sharper upper edges to the clouds to define the white, again blending it into the paint below with a stippling action of the brush. Stand back and check the overall effect, making any adjustments as necessary.

INDEX